# Solve It!

# SOLVE IT!

## A Perplexing Profusion
## of Puzzles

### JAMES F. FIXX

Doubleday & Company, Inc.
Garden City, New York

*Library of Congress Cataloging in Publication Data*

Fixx, James F
Solve it.

SUMMARY: Presents a collection of puzzles requiring
leaps of logic for their solution. Includes a set of
10 rules for problem solving.
1. Puzzles—Juvenile literature.   [1. Puzzles]
I. Title.
GV1493.F54      793.7′3
ISBN 0-385-13039-2 Trade
0-385-13040-6 Prebound
Library of Congress Catalog Card Number 77–25589

*For Betsy, Steven, John, and Paul,*
*who have given me more games, puzzles, and adventures*
*than they know*

# How This Book
# Came to Be

Back in 1972 I published a small book called *Games for the Superintelligent*. Because I had never done anything like it before (because, in fact, there *was* nothing quite like it anywhere), I had no idea what its reception might be. It was such a curious collection—not at all the usual puzzle book—that I wouldn't have been surprised if it had gone largely unnoticed. To my astonishment, it did nothing of the kind. Instead, a sizable band of *Games for the Superintelligent* devotees quickly sprang up. Reflecting on it, I came to realize that this company of puzzle lovers, consisting of all sorts of people from students to taxi drivers, from corporate executives to imprisoned felons, was bound together chiefly by the belief that the play of the human mind is the world's most exciting adventure. But it was linked, too, by another bond: the cheering discovery that other people shared the passion for thinking— a passion so pleasantly insistent that not long afterward a sequel, *More Games for the Superintelligent*, came into being.

In writing these two books I had in mind mainly adult readers. Although I never consciously excluded young people, it was grown-up puzzle lovers, people much like myself, that I was chiefly writing for. After the books appeared, however, I couldn't help noticing an odd contradiction. Some of the most perceptive comments about them came not from adults at all but from young people, many of whom clearly possessed minds significantly more flexible and wide-ranging than those of the typical adult. Nor could I help noticing that my own children—the same Betsy, Steven, John, and Paul to whom this book is dedicated—were among the most devoted readers and knowledgeable critics.

It was therefore only natural that the idea of doing a similar book especially for young people began to grow in my mind. When, one day, my publisher expressed the same thought, there was no resisting it; I set to work at once. This book is the result.

*Solve It!* is not, as you will quickly see, an ordinary book. Unlike most puzzle books, it is specifically written with young people of above-average intelligence in mind. While some of the problems in it aren't really very difficult (and some, once you understand their secrets, are downright easy), most require an interesting logical leap of one sort or another. For the most part, that is to say, they are puzzles that can't be solved by hard work alone. Rather, they call into play an ability to perform mental gymnastics.

The reason for that characteristic, I will confess, is not at all mysterious: that has long been my favorite kind of puzzle. If it's yours too, a warm welcome. You've come to the right place.

*J.F.F.*

# Contents

# *Solve It!*

# 1

# *The Pleasures*
# *of Problem Solving*

"I've got a problem!" What unpleasant thoughts those words bring to mind. Perhaps they recall the mental distress of some personal dilemma, of not being able to decide which way to turn or what to do next. Or perhaps they remind you of the frustration that makes you grind your teeth and chew the paint off your pencil as you grope for the solution to a tough question on a test in school.

Problems of that kind usually aren't a whole lot of fun. But there is another, different kind of problem that *is* fun, and that's the kind you'll find in this book. These are the problems that are deliberately calculated to stretch your mind, enlarge your understanding, strengthen your thought processes, and maybe—if they are particularly devilish—even trick you into stumbling down a dead end in order to see whether you can find your way out of it. But whatever the main purpose of such problems, they always have another purpose, too: to amuse and delight you with the sheer joy—and the incomparable rewards—of strenuous thinking.

All-out thinking brings two distinct kinds of fun.

First, there is the delight that comes simply from working on a problem, the fun of the thinking process itself. It can be the result of many things: of arriving at a solution so swiftly and so purposefully that you astonish yourself; of surmounting the confusion and helplessness you feel when you are momentarily convinced that a problem can't possibly be solved; or perhaps of thinking your way to a sudden insight that transforms a maddening complication into something so simple that you laugh out loud when you hit upon it.

Second, there is what has been described as "the thrill of success." Solving a tough problem can be just as rewarding as hitting a home run or sinking a difficult basketball shot. Scientists and inventors have written of the sense of excitement that comes as they suddenly find the solution to a problem that has been on their minds for a long time. This excitement, they report, is one of life's highest pleasures.

A homely illustration will show what I mean.

A few years ago a friend gave me a seemingly simple problem. You have a checkerboard, he said, from which two diagonally opposite squares have been removed:

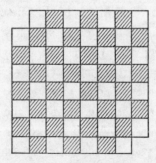

You also have thirty-one dominoes, each of which can cover two squares of the checkerboard. Can the dominoes be arranged so that they cover all sixty-two squares of the checkerboard? If so, how? If not, why not?

I'll bet that sounds easy to you. It did to me, too. Confidently, I got out a checkerboard and a set of dominoes. Placing the dominoes first this way and then that, I tried for some time to cover all the squares. No matter how hard I tried, however, I was unable to. Something always went wrong and I would wind up with isolated leftover squares. Before long I was at the edge of hopeless frustration.

Suddenly it occurred to me to try something different. What would happen, I wondered, if I were to use an altogether different tack? What if I assumed that the thirty-one dominoes could *not* be made to cover the sixty-two squares and set out to prove *that?* Thinking about it this way brought quite different results. It was, in fact, only a matter of minutes before I saw that 1) two diagonally opposite squares are always the same color, that 2) a domino must always cover two squares of *different* colors, and that 3) the problem therefore could not be solved because there would always be too few squares of one color or the other. The solution was so neat, so brief, and so elegant that it still gives me pleasure whenever I think of it.

Learning to solve problems like the ones in this book will give you bonuses beyond mere pleasure. Among other benefits, they will help you in your schoolwork and, later on, in whatever kind of work you decide to do. When, for example, two thousand computer programmers were asked to list their hobbies, it was found that those who spent time doing puzzles and playing logic games were the best at their jobs. A senior instructor at a government computer school in

Washington, D.C., told me, "You can hardly visit a computer center without being challenged to solve a puzzle."

If, then, puzzles not only bring us pleasure but also help us to work and learn more effectively, is it not worthwhile to learn to do them well? It certainly is. Fortunately, there are several ways to reach that goal.

Problem solving is not just a hit-or-miss process. There are four distinct stages. Moshe F. Rubinstein, a specialist in scientific problem solving at the University of California, describes them as follows:

*Stage 1: Preparation.* You go over the elements of the problem and study their relationship.

*Stage 2: Incubation.* Unless you've been able to solve the problem quickly, you sleep on it. You may be frustrated at this stage because you haven't been able to find an answer and don't see how you're possibly going to.

*Stage 3: Inspiration.* You feel a spark of excitement as a solution (or a possible path to one) suddenly appears.

*Stage 4: Verification.* You check the solution to see if it really works.

These four steps are exactly the ones many of the world's most gifted thinkers—scientists, mathematicians, inventors, and so forth—have followed in making some of history's significant discoveries. Merely to know what the steps are, however, is not necessarily the same as being able to follow them. To do that, we need a more detailed set of rules.

Such a set of rules follows. Actually, they are not so much rules as guidelines, for when it comes to thinking, there are very few unbreakable rules. If you keep these guidelines in mind, they will enable you to solve many problems, even very difficult ones. Since you'll be using them again and again, they are worth memorizing. For convenience, we can call them the "Scaredycat" technique because each rule begins with a successive letter of that word.

Here, step by step, are the ten rules of the Scaredycat technique, with a few explanatory comments about each:

*Rule 1: Study the question carefully.* Read the problem over, several times if you like, to be sure you understand exactly what is being asked. This is always an important rule, but it is particularly crucial if a question is complicated or if you have reason—as you will later on in Chapter 6—to suspect that an attempt is being made to trick you. Consider, for example, the following question:

> If an airplane crashes directly on the boundary between California and Oregon, where are the survivors buried?

If you are not alert to exactly what you are being asked, it may be quite some time before you abandon the *apparent* question and realize (with appropriate embarrassment) that we don't customarily bury people alive.

*Rule 2: Confidently start work.* In solving puzzles, a self-assured attitude is half the battle. When the confident person is momentarily stumped, he is not discouraged but presses ahead, certain that sooner or later a solution will come. Before you begin, it will help your self-confidence if you have at hand everything you're likely to need: pencils, paper, a ruler, scissors, and perhaps a dictionary to make sure you know the exact meanings of all the words in a problem. (If you mistake "radius" for "diameter," you're in trouble.) As you work, do so with purpose and energy. If one effort fails, move on to another. Above all, don't say, "That one's too tough for *me!*"

Chances are it only *looks* too tough and is readily solvable
once you discover the key. As your list of successfully solved
problems grows, so will your self-confidence. By the time
you've been through all the problems in this book, you'll be
virtually unstoppable.

*Rule 3: Appraise the context.* If you look closely, you can
often gather important clues from a problem's surroundings.
Consider, for example, this one, adapted from a puzzle that
appears in one of my earlier books:

> Two bicycles are approaching each other at a constant
> speed of ten miles an hour. When they are two miles
> apart, a bird leaves one bicycle and flies toward the other
> at a speed of fifty miles an hour. Upon reaching that bi-
> cycle, it immediately reverses direction. This continues
> until the bicycles meet. How far does the bird fly alto-
> gether?

At first glance, it appears that the only way to solve this problem is to add up the progressively smaller distances that the
bird covers as the two bicycles approach each other. But that,
an alert and thoughtful reader of my book would realize, was
a considerably tougher problem than I was likely to include,
especially since I myself am shaky with anything more complicated than elementary-school mathematics. It was a safe
guess, therefore, that there had to be an easier way to solve
the problem. And, sure enough, there *was:* Simply figure out
how long it is before the two bicycles reach each other (six
minutes) and calculate how much distance the bird covers in
that time (five miles).

Much the same reasoning can be applied to many of the
problems in this book, since—you have my word for it—

sound, logical reasoning is far more important than advanced mathematical ability. (In fact, as you will see in the discussion of Rule 6 below, too much mathematical sophistication may hurt rather than help.)

*Rule 4: Relax.* Sometimes intuition and imagination are more reliable allies than straightforward effort. A friend who is an excellent puzzle solver once referred to a "sideways style" of thinking—that is, one that approaches a problem from an unexpected direction. The sideways style comes most easily when we relax and don't press too hard. Relaxing is a particularly useful strategy when you feel frustrated by your inability to find a solution. There is an odd paradox in puzzle solving; trying too hard and caring too much are more likely to slow you down than speed you up. If, for a moment, you pretend that you don't really care, an answer may simply pop into your head.

*Rule 5: Expect to wait.* Not all problems, and certainly not all of those in this book, can be solved by hard work alone. Many depend on a sudden insight or inspiration. But inspiration is a curious and sometimes perverse thing; it doesn't always arrive when you need it most. André Marie Ampère, whose surname we have given to a unit of electrical current, once tried repeatedly to find a solution to a particular mathematical problem. Over a period of several days he returned to it again and again. Ampère describes how the answer finally came to him: "I had sought twenty times unsuccessfully for this solution. For some days I had carried the idea about with me continually. At last, *I do not know how,* I found it." This is the incubation period mentioned earlier. Where some problems are concerned, waiting is an inescapable part of the solution.

*Rule 6: Don't accept unnecessary limitations.* In a well-known problem you are asked to connect nine dots using four straight, connected lines:

Most people, when first confronted with this problem, are baffled. They make one attempt after another, but with no success. The reason for their difficulty is simple: They assume that they are not permitted to go outside the imaginary boundary created by the outer dots. Actually, of course, no such limitation has been expressed. As soon as you see that, the solution comes easily:

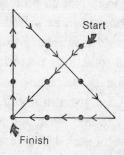

Sometimes, as mentioned, too much mathematical knowledge can create its own limitations. You are, of course, familiar with the idea of a series. If I were to ask you to give the next number in this list:

3, 6, 9, 12, 15, _____

you would have little difficulty in saying "18," since it is easy to see that each number is simply its predecessor plus three.

Not long ago in New York City I asked a friend who has had considerable mathematical training to tell me the next number in this series:

4, 14, 23, 34, 42, _____

He pondered, scribbled, wore a couple of pencils down to stubs, and finally got out his desk-top calculator—all to no avail. Finally, after he had shamefacedly given up, I pointed out that the numbers were those of the subway stops on the very line he rides to and from work every day! His mathematical expertise had made him look for a complicated answer rather than a simple one.

*Rule 7: Yesterday's problems may help.* Problems are very much like brothers and sisters. In some ways they may be very different from each other, but there are usually family resemblances. This is why, when you first encounter a problem, it's wise to ask yourself whether it's like any other problems you've seen. If, for example, you browse through books of puzzles in the library, you will invariably find problems in which some people always lie while others always tell the truth. Here is a typical example:

> A traveler comes to a fork in a road and doesn't know which way to go to reach his destination. There are two people at the fork, one of whom always lies while the other always tells the truth. The traveler doesn't know which is which. He is permitted to ask only one of the people one question to find his way. What is his question and which one does he ask?

Once you realize that the solution lies in asking two questions in one—for example, "If I were to ask you which road leads to Los Altos, which one would you say?"—the answer comes easily. And so do the answers to most other liar-and-truth-teller questions, since almost all of them (though not, just to make matters interesting, the two that appear later in this book) rely on exactly the same principle.

*Rule 8: Change the problem.* At the beginning of this chapter we looked at the problem of the checkerboard with two missing squares. You'll remember that when I was unable to prove that the dominoes *could* cover all the squares, I decided to try proving that they *couldn't*—and the answer came immediately. Changing a problem in that way is a valuable technique whenever you can use it. Sometimes, of course, you can't. In those cases, you simply have to push ahead in your original direction.

*Rule 9: Ask questions.* Although you will probably be working alone most of the time, there's no law that you must always solve problems without help. Sometimes, in fact, part of the fun comes from comparing ideas with others. Even if a friend or classmate can't actually solve a problem for you, he or she may point the way to a missing clue. You'll get the most satisfaction, of course, from solving a problem by yourself, but it's far better to use help than not to find a solution at all.

*Rule 10: Time brings all things.* Often we fail to solve problems because we aren't persistent enough. We give up before we've really begun. Many times you don't begin to understand a problem's real nature until you have become half convinced that it can't be solved at all. This happened to me not long ago when someone handed me this problem:

> Two people were talking. One said to the other, "I have three sons whose ages I want you to ascertain from the following clues:

a. The sum of their ages is thirteen.
b. The product of their ages is the same as your age.
c. My oldest son weighs sixty-one pounds."
"Stop," said the second person. "I know their ages."
What are they?

For a long time I couldn't get anywhere with that problem. What, I wondered, could the weight of the oldest son possibly have to do with anything? It wasn't until I had struggled for a long time that it occurred to me that the weight itself probably didn't matter at all and that the third clue might be telling me something entirely different. I was, of course, right.* There is no substitute for patience and persistence.

These, then, are ten rules that will serve you well in problem solving. They are not, needless to say, guaranteed to solve all problems, but they will greatly increase the likelihood of your finding a solution—and the likelihood, too, that you will experience what I referred to earlier as the thrill of success.

They are, in short, rules for getting more fun out of thinking. And that, I hope you'll agree, is what thinking, at its most rewarding, is really all about.

---

* The complete solution to the problem is wonderfully satisfying. There are only fourteen combinations of ages that correspond with the first and second clues. Since the person solving the puzzle presumably knows his own age, the fact that the second clue isn't sufficient to lead to a solution shows that his age must be thirty-six—the only product that occurs twice. The final clue, revealing that there is only one oldest son and not more, shows that the combination of ages cannot be 6, 6, and 1 but must be 9, 2, and 2.

# 2

# *Adventures in Logic*

Like the rest of this book, this chapter is intended to provide mental stimulation, challenges, and fun. Yet its real subject—the serious purpose behind all the mental frolicking—is the science of thinking. The reason is that logic, the mental faculty chiefly required in the exercises and amusements that appear in the next several pages, is the primary tool of thought.

Exactly what is logic? One dictionary defines it as "valid reasoning, especially as distinguished from invalid or irrational argumentation." The words *as distinguished from* are important ones, for very often valid and invalid reasoning look much alike. Consider this line of reasoning (it is technically called a syllogism):

> All water is wet.
> This is water.
> Therefore it is wet.

We instantly see that the conclusion—that is, the last of the three statements—is true; common sense alone tells us that. Now consider another set of statements, one that looks much the same:

All chickens have feathers.
This creature has feathers.
Therefore it is a chicken.

That conclusion, by contrast, is false. A simple diagram will show why:

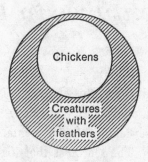

The sketch makes it clear that chickens are merely a *part* of the whole category of creatures with feathers. If a creature has feathers, therefore, the most we can be sure of is that it *may* be a chicken, not that it necessarily *is* a chicken.

As this example shows, it is easy to be tricked in problems involving logic. One false step and an entire solution collapses into meaningless pieces. Not many of the problems in this chapter require the use of formal syllogisms like those above, but they all require some form of "valid reasoning, especially as distinguished from invalid or irrational argumentation." That is why they provide a particularly appropriate introduction to the rest of the puzzles in this book.

Don't be discouraged if an answer doesn't come to you at once; it's not supposed to. And if at any point you find yourself absolutely stumped, go back and review the problem-solving rules in Chapter 1.

Above all, remember that puzzles are meant to be entertainment. Enjoy yourself.

## 1. Trying Trip

A parked car is facing west on a straight road. You get in and start driving. After traveling for a while, you find that you are a mile *east* of your starting point. Why?

## 2. Uncanny

You have two cans filled with water and a large empty container. Is there a way to put all the water into the large container so that you can tell which water came from which can?

## 3. Turnaround

A man in uniform was running home. Suddenly he saw a second man wearing a mask and holding a dread object. He quickly turned around and ran back to where he had come from. What familiar event was occurring?

## 4. Fish Story

Two fathers and two sons went fishing. Each person caught a fish, but they brought only three fish home with them. Why?

## 5. Which Is Which?

A boy and a girl are talking.
"I'm a boy," says the one with black hair.
"I'm a girl," says the one with red hair.
If at least one of them is lying, which is which?

## 6. Secret Formula

What is weightless, can be seen with the naked eye and, if put in a barrel, will make the barrel weigh less?

### 7.  Sporting Propositions

In what three sports does the winner cross the finish line backwards?

### 8.  Photographers and Cannibals

Three *National Geographic* photographers and three cannibals are traveling together through a jungle when they come to a river. The largest boat available can carry only two people at a time. The photographers are safe only if there are equal numbers of photographers and cannibals on each side of the river or more photographers than cannibals; otherwise, the photographers become dinner. How can they all get across?

### 9.  True or False?

You know that the inhabitants of Jamais always lie while the inhabitants of Toujours always tell the truth. You meet a man who you know comes from either Jamais or Toujours. You wish to know which village he comes from. How can you find out by asking him only one question?

### 10.  Changing the Odds

In a distant kingdom lived a king who had a beautiful daughter. When the daughter fell in love with a humble peasant boy, the king was shocked and upset. To show his fairness, however, he promised to let the peasant boy choose one of two slips of paper. On one would be written MARRIAGE and on the other DEATH. The peasant boy, eager for a chance to marry his beloved, agreed. As he was approaching the castle, he chanced to overhear a conversation between the king and one of his attendants.

"Sire," said the attendant, "how could you give this unworthy commoner a chance to marry the beautiful princess?"

"Have no fear," replied the king. "On both slips will be written the word DEATH."

The peasant boy was a clever youth. Instantly he saw a solution. Later that day he and the princess were married.

What was his solution?

## 11. Ninety Per Cent Right

Ten people, all wearing hats, were walking along a street when a sudden wind blew their hats off. A helpful boy retrieved them and, without asking which hat belonged to which person, handed each person a hat. What is the probability that exactly nine of the people received their own hats?

## 12. Shake

Is the number of people in the world who have shaken hands with an odd number of people odd or even?

## 13. Crime and Confusion

One of four girls has emptied a cookie jar. Their statements are as follow:

> ALICE: "Betsy did it."
> BETSY: "Martha did it."
> BARBARA: "I didn't do it."
> MARTHA: "Betsy lied when she said I did it."

If only one statement is true, which of the girls took the cookies?

## 14. Party Time

At a party of truth-tellers and liars you meet a new friend.

He tells you he has overhead a conversation in which a girl revealed her identity, saying she was a liar. Is your new friend a liar or a truth-teller?

## 15. Look Again

Where do you often see the fraction $^{24}/_{31}$?

# 3

## *Journeys into Space*

I have always treasured a quotation I once came across. It reads: "A genius is someone who shoots at something nobody else can see—and hits it." This is, it seems to me, a fascinating definition and an excellent one, but only so far as it goes. For there is among us today a special breed of genius that shoots at things practically nobody else can even *imagine*.

I am thinking of the scientists who send probes to the moon, to Mars, and into the far reaches of space. Few undertakings are more complex. Consider even a comparatively simple shot: to the surface of our next-door neighbor, the moon. First of all, the platform from which the launch is to be made—our own seemingly immobile Earth—is in fact very much in motion. It is not only spinning but is, at the same time, moving through space. Nor is its motion a straight line, or even a tidy circle. It is a sun-circling ellipse, an egg-shaped course that alternately speeds up and slows down. Secondly, the ellipse itself is continually changing position in space. Thirdly, the target—the moon—is traveling around Earth not in anything like a circle but in another ellipse. Furthermore, to complicate the aiming problem, in the moon's ellipse there are various bumps, wiggles, and wobbles. For you and me it would be virtually impossible to calculate where our bumping, wiggling, wobbling satellite is going to be several days from now, let alone to have the faintest hope of hitting it.

Yet hit it the scientists do. Their efforts are, of course, vastly aided by computers and other complicated devices. Still, the achievement is theirs. That achievement depends, among other things, on a highly developed ability to visualize space and the interrelationships of objects. As it happens, this is exactly what the puzzles in this chapter are mostly about. They require a sense of line, pattern, dimension, and motion. Not everybody is good at this kind of puzzle. Some people are quite skillful at mathematical problems but dismal at ones that require a spatial sense. Other people can do verbal puzzles—such as those in the next chapter—but have little sense of space. You may find, therefore, that these are harder for you than those in the preceding chapter. On the other hand, you may find that they are easier. Whatever the case, don't worry; the difficulties in this book all tend to balance out in the end.

### 1. Making a Point
Using only two straight lines, make a third arrow:

## 2.  The Upside-down Triangle
By moving only three coins, turn the triangle upside-down:

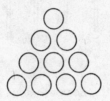

## 3.  Border Crossing
Beginning at the dot, draw a continuous line that crosses every segment of line exactly once:

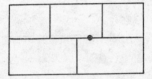

## 4.  Buggy
A set of encyclopedias consists of volumes that have ⅛-inch covers and one inch of pages. The set is arranged in order on a shelf. If a bookworm starts at the first page of Volume I and eats its way through to the last page of Volume II, how far does it travel?

## 5.  Match Game
Using six identical matches, make exactly four equilateral triangles. (An equilateral triangle has sides of equal length.)

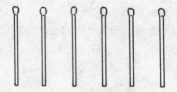

## 6. Lineup

Draw this figure with one continuous line—no retracing:

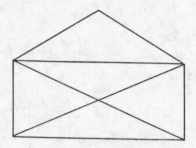

## 7. Scissors Trick

Trace the figure below. Do *not* cut the page. Then make one cut in Figure 1 so that you can rearrange the pieces to form Figure 2:

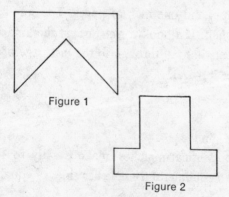

Figure 1

Figure 2

## 8.  Where There's a Will

A father wishes to divide a square piece of land among his five sons. One son is his favorite, and he wants to give him one quarter of the land, as shown:

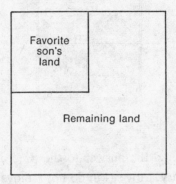

How can he divide the remaining land into four plots of equal size and shape?

## 9.  Lines and Circles

Using one continuous line and going over each portion once, create this figure:

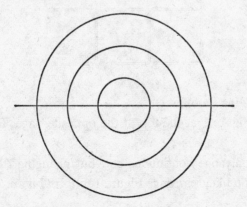

## 10. Square Deal

Move three matches to create three equal squares. (You must use all twelve matches.)

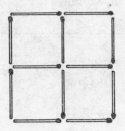

## 11. Try Again

If you discovered the answer to the preceding puzzle, this one should be easy. Move (but do not *re*move) three matches to leave only five squares.

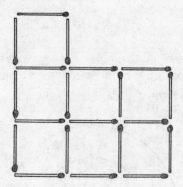

## 12. Puzzling Patterns

Trace Figure 1 at the top of the opposite page. Do *not* cut the page.

Using only one continuous cut, but changing direction as often as you like, rearrange Figure 1 to form Figure 2.

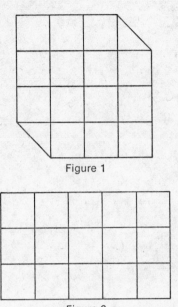

Figure 1

Figure 2

## 13. Rope Trick

Is it possible to pick up a piece of rope, one hand holding each end, and tie a knot in the rope without letting go of either end?

## 14. Overlapping Squares

Draw the following figure with one continuous line. You are permitted to cross lines but you may not go over any line more than once.

# 4

# *Words Both Weird and Wonderful*

When psychologists—the specialists who investigate the workings of the human mind—want to find out how bright a person is, they usually give him an I.Q. test. I.Q., which stands for "Intelligence Quotient," represents the difference between a person's mental age and his chronological age. If, for example, you are twelve years old but are as intelligent as the typical thirteen-year-old, you are said to have a high I.Q. If your mental age is exactly the same as your chronological age, you are said to have a normal I.Q., designated as 100.

Psychologists have devised a great many I.Q. tests, depending on their views of what intelligence is and how it can most reliably be measured. Some of these tests emphasize mathematical skill. Some rely heavily on abstract reasoning. Some require that your sense of spatial relationships—the sense you used so much of in the preceding chapter—be highly developed. In one respect, however, almost all I.Q. tests are alike: In one way or another, they all test your ability with words.

There are two main reasons for the psychologists' interest in how well you use words.

First, if you have a large and varied vocabulary, it's a sign that you have read a lot and have paid attention to what you have read. To enjoy reading is in itself an important sign of intelligence.

Second, an ability not just to *understand* words but to *use* them accurately and creatively is an indication that your mind is an efficient tool of thinking.

Thus the puzzles in this chapter are not simply fun and nothing else. On the contrary, they will give you some important insights into the way your mind works. Although a few of them test your knowledge of individual words, success in most of them depends upon your reasoning powers—and, in one or two cases, on a bit of intuition and luck.

## 1.  Footnote

Rearrange the letters in *elation* to spell a part of the body.

## 2.  Whats Up?

This is an unusual month—Santa, snow, and so on. This is an unusual paragraph, too. How quickly can you find out what is so uncommon about it? It looks so ordinary that you may think nothing is odd about it until you match it with most paragraphs this long. If you put your mind to it and study it you will find out, but nobody may assist you; do it without any coaching. Go to work and try your skill at figuring it out. Par on it is about half an hour. Good luck—and don't blow your cool.

## 3.  Reversals

Name three six-letter words that become different words when their letters are reversed.

**4.  Sense from Nonsense**
Punctuate the following:

    a.  It was and I said not but
    b.  Time flies you cannot they pass by at such irregular intervals
    c.  Woman without her man is a brute

**5.  Vowel Play**
What ordinary English word contains all the vowels, including *y*.

**6.  Fore and Aft**
What do you find at the front of a wren but at the back of a crow?

**7.  Magic Number**
Add three lines to this number to turn it into a traveling man:

$$1030$$

**8.  Pronoun Game**
A pronoun is a word, such as *him* or *yours,* that stands for a person, place, or thing, or that forms its possessive. Name ten pronouns, ranging in length from one to ten letters.

**9.  Phunny Stuph**
In English, the letters *ph* are almost always pronounced as if they were *f.* Can you think of any words in which this is not true?

**10.   Spelling Bee**

What word is spelled wrong in every dictionary?

**11.   Alphabet Soup**

Put the rest of the alphabet in its proper place:

A      EF  HI  KLMN
  B  D    G   J
    C                    O

**12.   Countdown**

Read this sentence:

FINISHED FILES ARE THE RESULT OF YEARS OF SCIEN-
TIFIC STUDY COMBINED WITH THE EXPERIENCE OF MANY
YEARS.

How many times does the letter F appear? Count them only
once. Do not go back and count them again.

**13.   Love Letter**

What sentimental message does the following convey?

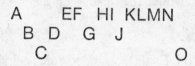

S   MMERS

**14.   Rhymeless**

Only a few English words have no rhymes. Can you name
three of them?

**15.   Case of the Vacationing Vowels**

What English word contains no vowels?

## 16.  Oldie

RAILROAD CROSSING—LOOK OUT FOR THE CARS. Can you spell it without any R's?

## 17.  Triplets

Name ten parts of the body that are spelled with three letters each.

# 5

## *Going Mad with Math*

Mathematics, as we all know, is part of practically every aspect of our lives. We wake up in the morning to the sound of an alarm clock that divides the day into various mathematically derived parts and subparts. We go to school on a bus designed by engineers who used slide rules, calculators, and computers; the school itself was designed by architects and engineers who used similar instruments. The lunch we eat was prepared for us on the basis of the mathematics of nutrition—our need for so many calories, so much of each mineral, and so many vitamins. After school, our sports events are timed, counted, and entered in record books that eventually come to be vast collections of numbers. So it goes all day long, until at bedtime we again set the alarm clock and turn out the light (perhaps to count sheep—still another mathematical exercise!).

We are so used to the mathematics of everyday life that we overlook much of it. We hardly need to think about whether the amount of money in our pocket is enough to buy something we need, even though such a question cannot be an-

swered without going through a mathematical operation—
subtraction. Similarly, it takes practically no effort to realize
that if we go to bed at ten o'clock and get up at seven the next
morning, we will have nine hours of sleep—yet that requires
another mathematical calculation.

Because mathematics is so common a part of our lives, we
are easily fooled or baffled by problems that appear ordinary
but in some way are slightly out of the ordinary. That, mainly,
is what this chapter consists of. No deliberate effort is made to
mislead or to trick you. Yet all the questions have some quality that gives them a special interest, a fascinating difficulty,
or an amusing peculiarity. Once you have figured out, for
each question, what that quality is, the rest is easy.

One example will explain what I mean.

Suppose you and a friend want to see how fast each of you
can ride a bicycle. You have only one bicycle, so first your
friend pedals from Mile 1 to Mile 10 on a level road with you
on the back of the bicycle timing him. Then you pedal from
Mile 10 to Mile 20 while he times you. Although you know
you are quite evenly matched, for some reason your friend
wins easily. What is the reason?

Most people spend a lot of time trying to figure out what
conditions might have accounted for the difference. It is only
after quite a while that it finally occurs to them to examine the
distance covered—and when they do so they realize that the
two riders covered different distances! The *answer* is simple; it
is only the *question* that is tricky.

So be on the alert. Your mathematical vigilance is about to
be severely tested.

## 1.  Warmup

Divide 30 by one half and add 10.

## 2. Dark Secret

A mile-long train is moving at sixty miles an hour when it reaches a mile-long tunnel. How long does it take the entire train to pass through?

## 3. The Missing Sheep

A farmer had seventeen sheep. All but nine broke through a hole in the fence and wandered away. How many were left?

## 4. All Wet

A recipe calls for four cups of water. You have only a three-cup and a five-cup container. How can you measure out four cups of water?

## 5. Scrambled Eggs

If one and a half hens lay one and a half eggs in one and a half days, how many eggs will three hens lay in eight days?

## 6. Arrangement

Arrange the digits 1, 2, 3, 4, 5, 6, 7, 8, 9, and 0 so that they add up to exactly 100.

## 7. Switch

The following equation, in Roman numerals, says that six plus two equal five. Can you correct it by moving only one line?

$$VI + II = V$$

### 8.   The Telltale Number

Write a ten-digit number so that the first digit tells how many zeroes there are in the number, the second how many ones, the third how many twos, and so forth.

### 9.   100 the Hard Way

Using only 9's write a number that equals 100.

### 10.   Something Fishy

A fish weighs ten pounds plus half of its weight. How much does it weigh?

### 11.   Postal Perplexity

U.S. postage stamps are currently available in the following denominations: 1 to 16 cents, 18 cents, 20 cents, 21 cents, 24 cents, 25 cents, 30 cents, 40 cents, and 50 cents (plus $1 and a number of other higher denominations). What is the fewest stamps that will enable you to put the exact postage on a letter requiring anything from 1 cent to $1.01?

### 12.   Ticktock

A clock chimes every hour on the hour, and once each quarter hour in between. If you hear it chime once, what is the longest you may have to wait to be sure what time it is?

### 13.   The Waterlily Problem

Waterlilies on a certain lake double in area every twenty-four hours. From the time the first waterlily appears until the lake is completely covered takes sixty days. On what day is it half-covered?

## 14.  Symphony in Sevens
Make four 7's equal 56. You may add, subtract, multiply, or divide in any combination.

## 15.  Fanciful Fives
Now make four 5's equal 56.

## 16.  Square Deal
Arrange the numbers 1 to 9 so that the total is 15 when added horizontally, vertically, and diagonally.

## 17.  The Baffling Bicycle
A bicycle climbs a certain hill at 10 miles an hour and returns at 20 miles an hour. What is its average speed for the entire trip?

## 18.  Figure Eight
An eight-digit number contains two 1's, two 2's, two 3's, and two 4's. The 1's are separated by one digit, the 2's by two digits, the 3's by three digits, and the 4's by four digits. What is the number?

## 19.  The Balancing Brick
A brick balances evenly with three quarters of a pound and three quarters of a brick. What does the whole brick weigh?

## 20.  The Scrambled Salesman

An egg salesman was asked how many eggs he had sold that day. He replied, "My first customer said, 'I'll buy half your eggs and half an egg more.' My second and third said the same thing. When I had filled all three orders I was sold out and I had not had to break a single egg all day."

How many eggs had he sold in all?

# 6

## Pure Skulduggery

Some readers will hate this chapter. Others will enjoy it more than any other in the entire book. The reason is that in all these puzzles a deliberate attempt is made to mislead you —and people either love such trickery or can't stand it.

These puzzles reveal an interesting fact about the way the human mind works: Most of the time, we see what we expect to see and hear what we except to hear, regardless of what is actually there.

A familiar example will show what I mean:

> If an electric train is going west at sixty miles an hour and the wind is blowing from the north at thirty miles an hour, in which direction will the smoke from the engine blow?

Reading this, most people assume that the question asks exactly what it *seems* to ask. Thus they take up their paper and pencil and start sketching and figuring. What they often overlook, at least at first, is that electric engines don't produce any smoke! They have been tripped up not by what is actually expressed, but by what they *expect* to see expressed.

So be forewarned. This chapter is a battle of wits in which the puzzles try, by means both fair and foul, to fool you, while you try to stay clear of their booby traps.

Can you win the battle?

### 1. Profound Question
If it takes seven men seven days to dig seven holes, how long will it take one man to dig half a hole?

### 2. Play Ball
There are nine men on a baseball team. How many outs are there in an inning?

### 3. Small Wonder
What's between heaven and earth?

### 4. Think Again
Here are four marks:

Put down five more marks and make ten.

### 5. Rendezvous
A car in Philadelphia starts toward New York City at 40 miles an hour. Fifteen minutes later a car in New York starts toward Philadelphia—90 miles away—at 55 miles an hour. Which car is nearest Philadelphia when they meet?

### 6. Playing Post Office
How many three-cent stamps are there in four dozen?

### 7. Snooze

If you went to bed at eight o'clock at night and set the alarm to get up at nine the next morning, how many hours of sleep would you get?

### 8. Bird Baffler

Is it possible to put 46 parakeets into nine cages so that each cage contains an odd number of parakeets?

### 9. Pig Problem

Now put nine pigs into four pigpens so that an odd number of pigs are in each pen.

### 10. Hike

Assume that you walk at a speed of three miles an hour. If a two-mile-wide forest has a two-mile trail leading directly through it, how far into the forest can you go in half an hour?

### 11. Look Hard

What word in this chapter is mispelled?

### 12. Pole Puzzle

You are an Army captain with one sergeant and four men at your command. You must put a 100-foot flagpole into a 10-foot hole. You have two ropes—one 10 feet long and the other 22 feet long—and a candle. How do you accomplish the task?

### 13. The Perplexed Patient

If a doctor gave you nine pills and told you to take one every half hour, how long would they last?

### 14. Groovy

A phonograph record is 12 inches in diameter. The diameter of the unused portion in the center is 3½ inches. The smooth outer band is ¼ inch wide. The grooves containing the music are spaced 30 to the inch. How far does the needle move as the record plays?

### 15. Splat

A stepladder is placed on a cement floor. You stand on the stepladder holding a raw egg, intact in its shell, and drop the egg six feet. It does not break. Why?

### 16. Look! Up in the Air!

What do you call creatures that fly and have four legs?

### 17. Wrong Number

Thirteen per cent of the people in a certain town have unlisted phone numbers. You select three hundred names at random from the phone book. What is the expected number of people who will have unlisted numbers?

# 7

## *Just for Fun*

Thus far we have been dealing mainly with more or less difficult problems—puzzles that require you to think hard, use all your wits and intuition, and stick at your assigned task in spite of setbacks and frustrations.

This chapter is intended as an intermission, a break from all the heavy thinking you've been doing. It's here for only one reason: for the pure fun of it.

Where games are concerned, fun is the most legitimate of all purposes. The earliest civilizations, just as eager for fun as we ourselves are, played games. If you visit the Metropolitan Museum of Art in New York City, you will see games that were played thousands of years ago by the inhabitants of ancient Egypt. Games have been a part of human history for so long that many different types have evolved. There are board games, such as checkers, chess, and Monopoly; outdoor games like football, baseball, and jumping rope; indoor games like Ping-Pong and darts; and scores of others.

Those in this chapter fall into several categories, yet they have one thing in common: they are all games that appeal to bright people. They are, each in their special way, difficult games, but their difficulties are balanced by a very clear reward: the sheer joy of thinking hard.

My children and I have long been game players, and we have spent many hours playing those in the following pages. We've had lots of fun with them. I think you will too.

## 1.  Car Game

In many states automobile license plates bear several letters, usually combined with numbers. In California, for example, a friend of mine reports having seen such combinations as:

DGM
FXH
JIW
MZP
ZTE
TJE

The object of this game is to think of words containing such letters in order. For the ones given, solutions might be:

DiaGraM
FoXHole
JIgsaW
MarZiPan
ZiThEr
TraJEctory

As you go down the highway, jot down the first ten combinations you see. The first person to find words to fit all ten wins.

## 2. Car Game No. 2

Here's another license-plate game. This is how its origina-
tor, Frank Reinking of Dallas, Texas, describes it:

> Notice a license plate and remember the digits on it.
> Then determine how many consecutive numbers (1, 2, 3,
> 4, and so forth) you can form by addition, subtraction,
> multiplication, and division, using each digit only once.
> For instance, let's say a license plate contains the number
> 1, 4, 6, and 7. Using those digits, we can get:

| | | |
|---|---|---|
| $1=1$ | $6=6$ | $7+4=11$ |
| $6-4=2$ | $7=7$ | $7+4+1=12$ |
| $7-4=3$ | $7+1=8$ | $7+6=13$ |
| $4=4$ | $6+4-1=9$ | and so forth. |
| $4+1=5$ | $6+4=10$ | |

The object is to see how far you can get before you can't
think of any more combinations.

## 3. Rules of the Game

In this amusing and baffling game, you challenge your
friends simply to discover its rules. To do so, they are permitted to ask questions that can be answered with a "Yes" or a
"No." The interesting aspect of this game is that the meaning
of a question has absolutely no bearing on anything.

Are you confused?

Actually, it's all quite simple. If a question ends with the
letters A through M, you answer "Yes." If it ends with N
through Z, you answer "No."

For example, let's suppose you are asked, "Are you lying?"
In that case, you would answer "Yes." But if you are asked,
"Are you telling the truth?" you would also answer "Yes."

The first person to discover the rules wins.

## 4. Magic Numbers

This is a good way to mystify a friend. Ask someone to pick a number, any number at all, but not to tell you what it is. Have him silently multiply it by five, add five to the product, multiply the resulting number by two, add two to it, and tell you the result. Instantly you are able to tell him the number he started with.

The secret: To find the number selected, simply delete the last digit from the number given to you. Then subtract one from the remaining number.

Can you figure out why this works as it does?

## 5. Outguess Your Opponent

This is a game in which each of two players tries to outguess the other. All you need are the spade, club, and heart suits of a deck of cards. Kings count 13, queens 12, and jacks 11. Aces count 1. All other cards count their face value. The object is to win the greatest number of hearts.

To start, one player takes the spade suit and the other the club suit. The hearts are shuffled, cut, and placed face down in a stack between the players. Then the heart at the top of the stack is turned face up.

Now each of the players chooses a card and places it face down on the table. Both players then turn their cards over, and the player with the higher card wins the heart. The sequence is repeated until all thirteen tricks have been played.

Each spade or club may be played only once, and all cards are left face up after having been played, in order to eliminate any advantages of memory. Forty-six heart points win. If there is a tie on a play, the value of that card is split.

The secret of the game is to try to guess what card your opponent will play and then either to beat him by only one point or lose by a lot. It's harder than it sounds, since your opponent is trying to do exactly the same thing to you.

### 6. Your Move

Did you ever notice that most business firms aren't located where their names suggest they should be? Shouldn't Goodyear really be in Wheeling, West Virginia? And shouldn't the Pet Rock company be in Boulder, Colorado, Revlon in Kissimee, Florida, and Gallo Wines in Portland, Oregon?

How many other companies can you put in their proper places? Try it with a friend and see who can do the most rearranging in fifteen minutes.

### 7. Outsider

Here's a good game to play when there is one new member in a group. Everyone except the new person knows the secret. The object is for the new person to discover what the game is and how it is played. He or she may try to do so by directing questions to any members of the group in any order.

All members of the group sit in a circle. Any question may be asked, and all questions must be answered truthfully—at least truthfully under the rules.

The secret of the game is that all questions are answered as if they had been directed to the person immediately to the left of the person who was actually asked.

Amusing situations invariably arise. For example:

QUESTION: "Are you wearing a red shirt?"

ANSWER: "No." (When the person *is* wearing a red shirt.)

*Or:*

QUESTION: "Where do you live?
ANSWER:    "I'm not sure. On Elm Street, I think."

*Or:*

QUESTION: "How many brothers and sisters do you
           have?"
ANSWER:    "I don't know."

## 8.  Three Words

This is a fascinating—and sometimes extremely difficult
—word game for two or more people.

One person gives a word. Let's say it is *read*. Now another
person thinks of a word closely associated with it—such as
*page*—but does not say it aloud. He then thinks of a third
word that is closely associated with the second word—such as
*boy*—and says it out loud.

The object is for the other player or players to guess the
second word.

Some sample combinations:

*Clock—tick—bug.*
*Horse—tail—Snow White and the Seven Dwarfs.*
*Beard—hair—rabbit.*

## 9.  Inventions

This is a game my children and I made up and have played
for years. We've found it an excellent one to amuse ourselves
with while relaxing on a rainy day or taking a long hike.

It's played this way:

One person names three totally unrelated objects—for example, an old inner tube, a flashlight, and a mouse.

Another person must think of a use for the three objects, the more fanciful the better. For the three objects cited above, he might say, "This can be made into a device for capturing owls for zoos. Release the mouse in a forest at night and wait until an owl lands nearby, intent on devouring it for supper. Shine the flashlight in the owl's eyes to blind it momentarily. While the startled owl wonders what to do, wrap the inner tube around the helpless bird like a strait jacket."

A friend of mine who specializes in teaching bright children says this is an excellent game for encouraging creativity. Maybe so. But for me and Paul, John, Betsy, and Steven, the main thing is that it's so amusing and, much of the time, so wonderfully silly.

# 8

## Games for
## the Supersuperintelligent

The puzzles in this chapter are the most difficult in the entire book. Some, in fact, are harder than many that appear in the books I have written for adults.

Thus you may well ask: What are puzzles like these doing in a book intended for young people?

The reason is simple. They are here because, tough as they are, this is exactly where they belong. As a whole, young people have much more flexible minds than adults do, and they are quicker to find inventive solutions. Most important, they are usually not discouraged by questions that appear to be extremely difficult.

Chances are that if you've already worked your way this far into the puzzles in this book, you're well prepared for the problems in this chapter. Don't worry if you can't do some of them at first. They're tough; there's no question about that. But not a single one of them is beyond the ability of a bright young person—especially if you're willing to work hard.

So go to it, and good luck.

**1. Case of the Counterfeit Coins**

You have ten stacks of ten silver dollars each. They are identical, except that one stack consists entirely of counterfeit dollars. You know the weight of an authentic dollar, and you also know that a counterfeit dollar weighs one gram less. How many weighings are needed to reveal which stack is counterfeit?

**2. Going Around in Circles**

The three circles below are all the same size. How many circles will it take in all to make a complete ring around the shaded circle? Do this one without using coins or other circles, and prove your answer.

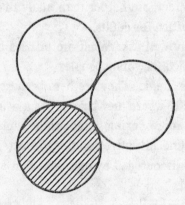

**3. Strange Series**

The following number is the only one of its kind. Can you figure out what is so special about it?

8,549,176,320

**4. Making Waves**

A rowboat is floating in a swimming pool. Which will raise

the water level more—dropping a rock into the water or putting the same rock into the boat? Or does it make any difference?

## 5. Boxed In

Three boxes contain two coins each. One contains two nickels, one contains two dimes, and one contains a dime and a nickel. All three boxes are mislabeled. If you are permitted to take out only one coin at a time, how many must you take out in order to be able to label all three boxes correctly?

## 6. Geography Lesson

Which state in the United States is the northernmost? The easternmost? The westernmost?

## 7. Weighty Question

Which weighs more, a pound of gold or a pound of lead?

## 8. Early Bird

A chauffeur always arrives at the train station at exactly five o'clock to pick up his boss and drive him home. One day his boss arrives an hour early, starts walking home, and is eventually picked up. He arrives at home twenty minutes earlier than usual. How long did he walk before he met his chauffeur?

## 9. Take a Letter

What three different digits are represented by X, Y, and Z in this addition problem?

$$\begin{array}{r} XZY \\ +XYZ \\ \hline YZX \end{array}$$

## 10.  Devious Dates

An author writes a book every two years. When his seventh book is published, the sum of the years in which they were all published is 13,804. In which years were his seven books published?

# 9

## *The Almost Official Mensa Intelligence Test*

Earlier in this book we took a brief look at I.Q.—the number that describes how intelligent a person is. We saw that a person of average intelligence is, by definition, exactly in the middle of the entire population; that is, the number of people more intelligent and less intelligent are the same. Most people are fairly close to average. It is clear, therefore, that if someone is so intelligent that only 1 or 2 per cent of the population is more intelligent, then he or she is very intelligent indeed.

This is exactly the case with members of Mensa, an organization whose only entrance requirement is that your intelligence put you in the top 2 per cent of the population. Mensa, started in 1945 in England, swiftly spread to the United States and other countries. Today there are 150 or so chapters in the United States alone, and their members consist of people of all ages.

Most Mensa members aren't the least bit snobbish about their high intelligence. They accept it just as they accept their height or the color of their eyes. They join Mensa not to brag about how smart they are but because they enjoy spending time with other people as intelligent as they are, people who share the same interests and hobbies. (Many Mensa members, incidentally, love puzzles like those in this book.)

To find out whether you yourself qualify for Mensa, you can write to their headquarters (Mensa, Department J, 1701 West Third Street, Brooklyn, N.Y. 11223) and ask for information on how to take the necessary tests. In case you're curious about whether you're likely to pass these tests, this chapter contains ten questions exactly like the ones Mensa uses. They were prepared by Mensa's psychologist, Dr. Max Fogel, and made available especially for this book. Answers and a scoring key appear at the back of the book.

### 1.  Gap
Fill in the missing number in the series:

   65, 33, ———, 9

### 2.  Telltale Two
Which two of the following words are the most similar in meaning?

    attract
    lure
    entice
    persuade
    please

### 3.  Turnabout
Which of diagrams *a*, *b*, *c*, and *d* can be either turned over or rotated to become the same as this diagram?

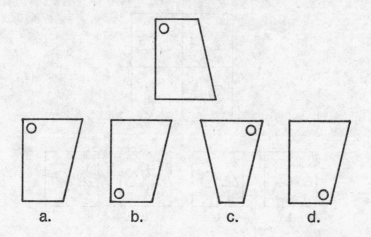

**4. Missing Number**

Complete the equation by inserting the same number in both places:

$$\frac{3}{(\quad)} = \frac{(\quad)}{27}$$

**5. Intruder**

Which word does not belong in the following list?

car
moon
fish
happy
belief

**6. Next**

Complete the diagram with either *a, b, c,* or *d:*

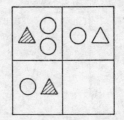

a.              b.              c.              d.

## 7. Hierarchy

M is above N and O

N is above O and below P

Therefore:

a. M is not over O and P

b. O is above N

c. P is above O

d. O is above P

## 8. Analogy

Complete the analogy by writing one word in the spaces, ending with the letters printed. Example: High is to low as sky is to /e/a/r/t/h/.

Skull is to brain as shell is to / / /l/k/.

## 9. Four Words

Complete this sentence by using one word from each of the four groups below:

_____(a)_____ we must continually _____(b)_____ our

knowledge by learning from the studies of others, we must never ____(c)____ the importance of observation of the ____(d)____ themselves.

    a. if, sometimes, when, while
    b. condense, believe, expand, begin
    c. postpone, exaggerate, prevent, forget
    d. studies, data, conclusions, observers

**10.  Squaring Off**

Complete the series with either *a, b, c,* or *d:*

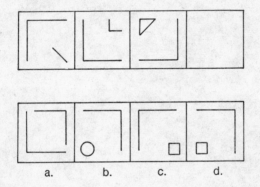

     a.        b.        c.        d.

# *The Helpers*

A book like this one is necessarily a collaborative effort since, over the years, a great many people have provided me not just with puzzles but with all manner of aid and counsel. Among them are the readers of the four magazines published by MBA Communications, Inc., for which I have written a monthly puzzle column since 1973; my colleagues at MBA; my wife, Alice; Carol Farris, as fine a typist as any author could wish for; the indefatigably inventive members of Mensa; and especially Martin Berl, Orville Brandes, Bill Broer, Margaret B. Capron, Alan R. Cohen, John D. Coons, Tom Crary, Darlene Criss, Katherine Dixon, Max Fogel, Hans G. Frommer, Marvin Grosswirth, Kevin E. Harold, R. A. Herold, Jerry E. Jackson, R. S. Johnson, John C. Klassen, John W. Knoderer, David Greene Kolodny, I. Jordan Kunik, Stephen H. Lampen, Leonard D. Lipner, Una Joyce McCormick, Leonard I. Meisel, Meredy Mullen, E. W. Paulson, E. E. Rehmus, Frank Reinking, Margot Seitelman, Marvin Smith, Art Swanson, Milton Van Dyke, and Philip G. Wik, all of whom helped in one important way or another. As always, the little old lady on Rose Street made her indispensable contribution.

*Answers to Puzzles*

## CHAPTER 2

**1.** The car was in reverse.

**2.** Yes. Freeze the water in the two cans before putting it into the empty container.

**3.** A baseball game was being played.

**4.** The hunters were a grandfather, a father and a son. The father was thus also a son.

**5.** The boy has red hair, the girl black hair. There are four possible combinations: true-true, true-false, false-true, and false-false. It is not the first, since we are told that at least one statement is false. Nor is it the second or third because, in each case, if one lied, then the other could not have been telling the truth. Therefore it is the fourth; both lied.

**6.** A hole.

**7.** Rowing, the backstroke, and the tug of war.

**8.** A cannibal and a photographer cross. The photographer returns. Two cannibals cross. One cannibal returns. Two photographers cross. One cannibal and one photographer return. Two photographers cross. One cannibal re-

turns. Two cannibals cross. One cannibal returns. Two cannibals cross.

**9.** Make it a nonsense question. "Are you a rhinoceros?"
will do just fine. Or ask a question whose answer you can ver-
ify, such as, "Is it raining?"

**10.** The peasant drew one of the slips of paper, quickly
tore it up, and threw the pieces away. Then he returned to the
king and said, "I have chosen my fate. Let us see which slip is
left."

**11.** The probability is zero. If nine people have their own
hats, then the tenth must too.

**12.** Even. The proof is as follows: If you were to ask everyone in the world how many hands he or she has shaken,
the total would be even because each handshake would have
been counted twice—once each by the two people who shook
hands. A group of numbers whose sum is even cannot contain
an odd number of odd numbers.

**13.** If you assume Alice is the criminal, Barbara's and
Martha's statements are true. If you assume Betsy is guilty,
Alice's, Barbara's, and Martha's statements are true. If you
assume Martha is the criminal, Betsy's and Barbara's state-
ments are true. Therefore Barbara is the criminal and only
Martha's statement is true.

**14.** A liar. A truth-teller cannot say she is a liar because
she cannot lie. A liar cannot say she is a liar because she cannot tell the truth. Therefore your new friend lied.

**15.** On calendars, when the 24th and 31st of a month are
squeezed into the same square.

CHAPTER 3

**1.**

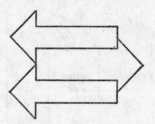

**2.**

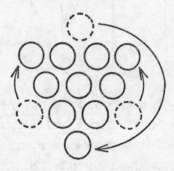

**3.**

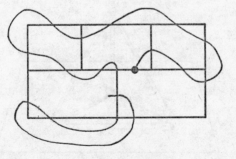

The solution is, of course, slightly sneaky. There is, however, no specific prohibition against *following* a line while not crossing it, as happens along the vertical line at the bottom of the diagram.

**4.**

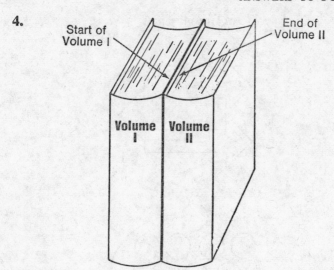

Only ¼ inch—the thickness of the two covers. Put a paper clip on the first page of one book, and another on the last page of a second book. Put both books on a shelf together and you will see why this surprising answer is correct.

**5.**

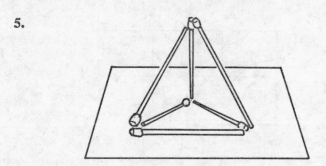

Those who have trouble with this one assume they must solve it in only two dimensions. Once you realize that the use of a third dimension is permissible, it's easy.

**6.**

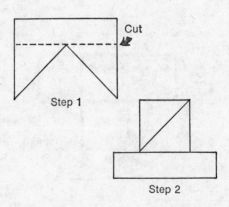

**7.**

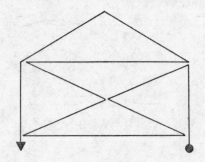

Cut

Step 1

Step 2

**8.**

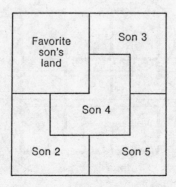

Favorite son's land

Son 3

Son 4

Son 2

Son 5

**9.**

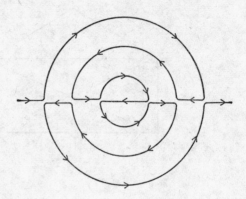

**10.**

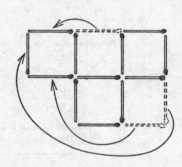

**11.**

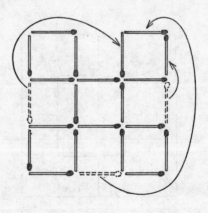

**12.**

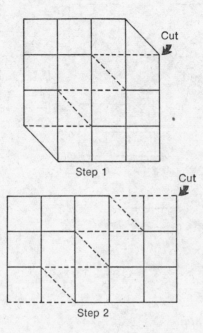

**13.**

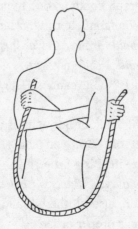

Yes. Fold your arms before you pick up the rope. Then simply pull your arms apart.

**14.**

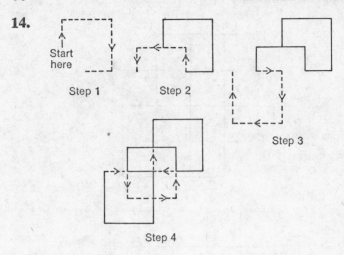

Step 1                    Step 2

Step 3

Step 4

CHAPTER 4

**1.** *Toenail.*

**2.** The paragraph contains one hundred words but not a single *e,* the most common letter in our language.

**3.** *Diaper, repaid; drawer, reward; spools, sloops.*

**4.** a. It was *and,* I said, not *but.*

b. Time flies? You cannot. They pass by at such ir-regular intervals.

c. Woman! Without her, man is a brute. (Or, depending on your point of view, you can simply add a period: Woman without her man is a brute.)

**5.** *Unquestionably. Facetiously* and *abstemiously,* though less common, also fill the bill and, as a bonus, contain all the vowels in their proper order.

**6.** The letter *w.*

**7.**

HOBO

**8.** *I, me, you, your, their, itself, herself, yourself, our-selves, themselves.* There are, of course, many others as well.

**9.** *Upheaval, upholster, uphold,* and so forth—wherever, in short, the *p* comes at the end of one syllable and the *h* at the beginning of the next.

**10.** *Wrong.*

**11.**      A      EF  HI  KLMN           T  VWXYZ
        B  D   G   J              PQR  U
          C                            O      S

The top row contains letters that are made up of straight lines; the middle row, letters formed by combinations of straight and curved lines; the third row, letters formed only by curves.

**12.** There are six F's. Because the F in OF sounds like V, many people overlook it. This is a good example of the ways we sometimes fail to see things as they really are because we are looking for the wrong things.

**13.** Summers without you (u) are (r) short and dark.

**14.** *Month, oblige,* and *orange.*

**15.** Nth.

**16.** "It." This, as many readers will realize, is a very old riddle. I myself first heard it from my father when I was barely old enough to read. It is included here because of the delight it always causes upon first encounter.

**17.** Rib, jaw, gum, hip, arm, leg, lip, eye, ear, and toe.

CHAPTER 5

**1.** 70. Dividing by one half *doubles* a number.

**2.** Two minutes—one minute for the engine and another minute for the last car.

**3.** Nine.

**4.** Fill the three-cup container and pour it into the five-cup container. Fill the three-cup container again and from it fill the five-cup container. Empty the five-cup container and pour the remaining cup from the three-cup container into it. Now fill the three-cup container and add it to the one cup that is already in the five-cup container. The result is the desired four cups.

**5.** Sixteen eggs. One hen lays one egg in one and a half days. Therefore three hens would lay three eggs in one and a half days, or two eggs in one day. Thus three hens would lay sixteen eggs in eight days.

| **6.** | 89 | *Or:* | 89 |
|---|---|---|---|
| | 7 | | 6 |
| | 5/2 | | 4 |
| | 4/3 | | 1/2 |
| | 1/6 | | 35/70 |
| | 0 | | 100 |
| | 100 | | |

**7.**

$$VI \mathrel{\raise{0.5ex}{\overset{\frown}{\;+\;}}} II = IV$$

**8.** 6,210,001,000

**9.** 99 $\frac{99}{99}$

**10.** Twenty pounds. The solution is arrived at as follows:

$$W = 10 + \tfrac{1}{2}W$$
$$W - \tfrac{1}{2}W = 10$$
$$\tfrac{1}{2}W = 10$$
$$W = 20$$

**11.** Seven. The stamps are: 1 cent, 2 cents, 4 cents, 8 cents, 16 cents, 30 cents, and 40 cents. For 1 cent in postage you need a 1-cent stamp. For two cents in postage, should you choose another 1-cent stamp or a 2-cent stamp? The answer is to take the 2-cent stamp, for two principles will guide you to the solution of this problem: 1) Don't take a new stamp unless you absolutely need it (that is, combine old ones first); and 2) when you do need a new stamp, choose the largest possible denomination.

**12.** An hour and a half—from 12:15 to 1:45. Once you have heard the clock chime once seven times, you need not wait for it to chime again, for the next cannot be anything but two o'clock.

**13.** The fifty-ninth day. Since the waterlilies double each day, the lake is half covered the day before it is fully covered. (Sometimes it is easier to solve a problem backward than forward.)

**14.** $7 \times 7\tfrac{7}{7}$

**15.** $55\tfrac{5}{5}$

**16.**

| 4 | 9 | 2 |
|---|---|---|
| 3 | 5 | 7 |
| 8 | 1 | 6 |

The square can, of course, be rotated in various ways. Mathematically, however, it remains the same in all four positions.

**17.** The apparent answer—15 miles an hour—is wrong. The correct answer is 13⅓ miles an hour because speed is determined by dividing distance by time. Notice, incidentally, that the answer is the same no matter how long the hill is.

**18.** 41,312,432

**19.** Three pounds. If the brick balances with three quarters of a brick and three quarters of a pound, then one quarter of a brick must weigh three quarters of a pound. Thus a whole brick weighs four times as much, or three pounds.

**20.** Seven. He sold four eggs to the first customer, two to the second, and one to the third. The problem is solved most easily if you start with the last customer and work forward.

CHAPTER 6

**1.** There is no such thing as half a hole.

**2.** Six—three for each team.

**3.** The word *and*.

**4.**

**5.** They are both at the same point when they meet.

**6.** Forty-eight.

**7.** Only one. The alarm would go off at nine o'clock the same night.

**8.** It certainly is. Put one parakeet into each of the first eight cages and 38 parakeets into the ninth cage. (Isn't thirty-eight parakeets an odd number to put into a single cage?)

**9.**

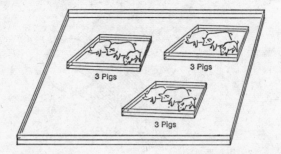

There are also other variations on this solution; all rely on using pens within pens.

**10.**   One mile. After that, you're coming *out* of the forest.

**11.**   *Misspelled*.

**12.**   You say, "Sergeant, get that flagpole up."

**13.**   Four hours. You take the first pill right away, not a half hour later.

**14.**   The needle traces a path from the inside of the outer smooth portion to the outside of the inner unused portion. Thus it travels 4 inches, plus slightly more since it actually moves in an arc.

**15.**   You were holding the egg seven feet from the floor. Thus it does not break until it has gone seven feet.

**16.**   Two birds.

**17.**   None. An unlisted phone number doesn't appear in the phone book.

## CHAPTER 8

**1.**   Only one. Weigh one coin from the first stack, two coins from the second, and so forth. The number of grams by which the total is light will correspond to the number of the counterfeit stack.

**2.**

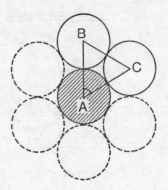

Exactly six circles will complete the ring. For the proof, inscribe the angle ABC in the center circle and two of the outer circles. The triangle is equilateral, since each side is equivalent to two radii. In equilateral triangles, each angle is 60°. Therefore Angle A is 60°, or one sixth of a 360° circle.

**3.** It is the only one that contains all the numerals in alphabetical order.

**4.** It does indeed make a difference. A submerged object displaces its volume, while a floating object displaces its weight. Since the rock is heavier than an equal volume of water (as proven by the fact that it will sink in water), putting it into the boat will raise the water level more.

**5.** Only one. Take it from the box labeled "Dime and Nickel." Since you know all three boxes are mislabeled, the box contains two coins of the denomination you withdrew. Put the proper label on that box. Then simply switch the two remaining labels.

**6.** Alaska is all three. Because the Aleutian Island chain, part of Alaska, extends across the 180th meridian into the eastern hemisphere, Alaska is both the easternmost and westernmost state.

**7.** A pound of lead. Lead is weighed in the standard measure, in which 7,000 grains equal a pound. Gold is measured in Troy weight, in which 5,760 grains equal a pound.

**8.** For fifty minutes. He saved the chauffeur ten minutes of traveling time each way and thus was picked up at 4:50 P.M. rather than the usual time.

**9.** X=4, Y=9, and Z=5. The solution need not depend entirely on trial and error. For example, since the X's in the left column do not add up to more than a one-digit number, they must be either 1, 2, 3, or 4. But since Y and Z in the right column cannot be the same numbers, the smallest numbers they can be are 1 and 2—in which case the X in that column would be at least 3. Therefore we know X is either 3 or 4. Now consider the left column again. Since we now know that X is either 3 or 4, Y must be 6 or greater. But we know that since Y and Z in the other two columns do not yield the same digit in both cases, Y and Z must equal at least 11 and therefore X plus X in the left column must be either 7 or 9. Similar reasoning in the case of Z reduces the need for trial and error still further, and the answer is easily arrived at.

**10.** The average of all seven years is the same as the middle year, the year the fourth book was published. Therefore 13,804 divided by 7 gives the middle year: 1972. There were thus three books earlier than that—in 1970, 1968, and 1966—and three books later—in 1974, 1976, and 1978.

*Scoring key:* If you get all ten right, you're a likely candidate for Mensa membership; seven or more, success is probable; less than seven, you'll have to pass the official Mensa test to find out.

## CHAPTER 9

**1.** 17. The pattern is as follows: Add 1 to a term and divide by 2 to get the next term.

**2.** *lure* and *entice*

**3.** *b*

**4.** 9

**5.** *Happy*—the only adjective. The other four words are nouns.

**6.** *a*

**7.** *c*

**8.** /y/o/l/k/

**9.** while, expand, forget, data

**10.** *d*

JAMES F. FIXX is a magazine editor and the author of *The Complete Book of Running*, *Games for the Superintelligent*, and *More Games for the Superintelligent*.